# ALL ABOUT THE MOON
## (Phases of the Moon)
## 1st Grade Science Workbook

Speedy Publishing LLC
40 E. Main St. #1156
Newark, DE 19711
www.speedypublishing.com

Copyright 2015

All Rights reserved. No part of this book may be reproduced or used in any way or form or by any means whether electronic or mechanical, this means that you cannot record or photocopy any material ideas or tips that are provided in this book

Each month our Moon passes through eight phases.

A new moon is when the side of the moon facing the Earth is not illuminated. The Moon and the Sun are lined up on the same side of the Earth, so we can only see the shadowed side.

Because the moon takes almost the same amount of time to complete one revolution as it does one rotation, we see mainly the same side of the moon at all times.

A waxing crescent moon is when the Moon looks like crescent and the crescent increases in size from one day to the next.

The first quarter moon means that the Sun and the Moon make a 90-degree angle compared to the Earth.

Gravity on the moon is only about 1/6 of that on Earth. If you drop a rock on the moon, it falls more slowly.

A waxing gibbous moon occurs when more than half of the lit portion of the Moon can be seen. The Moon remains in the sky most of the night.

The moon has its own time zone.

A full moon is when the Moon is brightest in the sky. This is also the time of the lunar month when you can see lunar eclipses.

A second full moon in one calendar month is usually called a "blue moon" and this occurs approximately every 3 years.

A waning gibbous moon is less than fully illuminated, but more than half.

The Earth, seen from the moon, also goes through phases.

The last quarter moon is when the Moon has reached half illumination.

A waning crescent moon is the final sliver of illuminated moon we can see before the Moon goes into darkness again.

The moon's orbit around Earth is an oval, not a circle, so the distance between the center of Earth and the moon's center varies throughout each orbit.

The moon is not round. Instead, it's shaped like an egg.

Tides on Earth are caused mostly by the moon.

Printed in Great Britain
by Amazon